GETTING UNSTUCK

A BEGINNER'S GUIDE TO TROUBLESHOOTING IN R

John S Bear

Makapuu Press

Published by Makapuu Press
ISBN: 979-8-9944546-0-2

Contents

Chapter 1

Why This Book?

R is a programming language. When using *any* programming language, it is necessary to know how to debug. Debugging is a skill that is most often learned in the school of hard knocks, but it can be taught.

When someone is new to R, there are a ton of things they don't know, and they don't even know what they don't know. That makes it hard to figure out what went wrong.

This book aims to remedy that with chapters explaining some of R's puzzling idiosyncracies, R's error messages, and some of R's built-in functions that are helpful for debugging. I also show

how to avoid some of the more common problems in the first place.

In addition, I describe a couple different strategies for finding the problem and fixing it, and then go through some examples showing how to apply the strategies.

In addition to the knowledge side, there is also the emotional side. Frustration is a real thing. So is anxiety. And both can rear their ugly heads when we get stuck—when the code looks exactly right, but the wrong thing is happening.

One of the goals of this book is to help you change your *emotional* reaction, when you see an error message, from a frazzled, "Oh crap!" to a calm, "Cool, this error message from R is helping me figure out how to do the right thing. Soon I'll have it fixed!"

That's why the very next chapter is on error messages, and why there are exercises at the end of the chapter, with answers. You'll also find a set of exercises with answers at the end of Chapter 3.

Chapter 2

A Gentle Introduction to Errors

In R, when something goes awry, we get an *error*, or a *warning*. An *error* happens when something goes so wrong that R cannot continue the computation. A *warning* is a message that says something is not being done the way it should be, but the computation can still continue.

When you get a warning, you're not really stuck. When you get an error, you are. In this book I'm concerned with helping you get unstuck, so I'm going to skip over warnings, and just deal with errors.

Error messages and warnings often contain words with special meanings. *Symbol* and *object* are two commonly occurring examples. A symbol is a name, like the name of a variable or function. *Object* comes from *object-oriented programming.* Most data structures in R are objects, so when an error message mentions an object, it is most likely referring to some data structure, like a vector, matrix, list, or data frame.

Knowledge of these technical terms provides the necessary foundation for beginning our quest to parse and understand error messages. The goal is to transform these messages from annoying gobbledygook into helpful and informative assistance.

2.1 When an Object Is Not Found

In programming texts, printing "hello world" is a common first example. We start with something even simpler, just printing "hello" to the screen (Example 2.1.1).

Example 2.1.1

```
> print(hello)
```

```
Error in print(hello) : object 'hello'
not found
```

In Example 2.1.1, when the interpreter tells us there is an object not found, that means it thinks `hello` is a variable, and R cannot find the object that is `hello`'s value. If, instead of `print(hello)`, we had tried `print(letters)`, things would have turned out better, because `letters` is a variable bound to the list of lowercase English letters. (See Example 2.1.2.)

Example 2.1.2

```
> print(letters)
 [1] "a" "b" "c" "d" "e" "f" "g" "h" "i"
[10] "j" "k" "l" "m" "n" "o" "p" "q" "r"
[19] "s" "t" "u" "v" "w" "x" "y" "z"
```

R interprets `letters` as a symbol, and prints the value of the variable named by that symbol. In our example, the function `print` is expecting a single thing to print, like a variable that has a value, or a constant vector, like `c(1,2,3)`, or `"hello"`. (The numbers in the output are explained in Chapter 7.)

One possibility is that we give `print` a *string constant* argument, like `'hello'`, with the single quotes, or `"hello"` with double quotes. *String constant* is from common computer science parlance, where people talk about a *string* of *characters. Constant* means not a variable. For instance, you can assign the value `"hello"` to the variable `myMessage`, but `"hello"` itself is a constant. In our case, in R, a string constant is any string of characters between single or double quotes. So each of the letters in Example 2.1.2 is a string constant. So is `"hello"`. So is `"hello world"`. We can fix Example 2.1.1 by putting single or double quotes around `hello`, as in Example 2.1.3.

Example 2.1.3

```
> print('hello')
[1] "hello"
```

To summarize, when you see an error saying something is "not found," R is probably encountering a name, and thinks it is a function or variable, and is failing to find the variable's value or the function's definition. Possible solutions are to put quotes around it if it should really be a string constant, or assign a value if it really should have one.

2.2 When Something Is Unexpected

Another extremely common and useful error message involves saying something is "unexpected" (Example 2.2.1).

Example 2.2.1

```
> print(pi)
[1] 3.141593
> print(pi, 2) # 2 is number of digits
[1] 3.1
> print(pi 2)
Error: unexpected numeric constant in
"print(pi 2"
```

In this example, the second argument to `print`, `2`, needs to be separated from the first argument by a comma. In the error, the phrase `numeric constant` is referring to the `2`. In general, in an error like this, the string of input that is returned, `"print(pi 2"`, stops at the first thing it cannot handle. That is `2` in this case. Compare Example 2.2.1 with Example 2.2.2. The inputs are different, but in both cases, the last part of the error is the same.

Example 2.2.2

```
> print(pi 2 4 6 8 )
Error: unexpected numeric constant in
"print(pi 2"
```

The string `"print(pi 2"` at the end of the error tells us that the problem has already happened by the time it reached `2`, i.e., before any of the later numbers. R stopped paying attention before it got to `4`, `6`, or `8`. That is important. A key strategy in troubleshooting is to figure out where the problem is. The error message in this case helps us eliminate any possibility after the `2`. In general, R uses commas to separate things like arguments to a function and elements of a vector. When you see an error with the word `unexpected` in it, one of the likely possibilities is that there is a missing comma somewhere. Unfortunately, it is not the only possibility. We cover another one in the next section.

2.3 When Delimiters Are Unexpected

Commas are a kind of delimiter—a way to separate different arguments of a function or elements of a vector or list. Parentheses, square brackets, double square brackets, and braces are also delimiters: `()`, `[]`, `[[]]`, `{}`. It is common for people, and not just beginners, to make mistakes with these delimiters. The error messages can be very helpful in finding and fixing them. In Example 2.3.1, the last thing quoted in the error message is the right brace immediately after `TRUE`.

Example 2.3.1

```
> if (TRUE} print('hi')
Error: unexpected '}' in "if (TRUE}"
```

And sure enough, the expression after an `if` needs to be surrounded by parentheses, not braces. Replacing the brace with a parenthesis fixes the problem (Example 2.3.2).

Example 2.3.2

```
> if (TRUE) print('hi')
[1] "hi"
```

In Example 2.3.3, the last element quoted in the error message is the left brace immediately after `print`.

Example 2.3.3

```
> if (TRUE) {print{'hi'}}
Error: unexpected '{' in
"if (TRUE) {print{"
```

Functions, like **`print`**, need to have their arguments surrounded by parentheses, not braces. Using parentheses fixes the problem, as shown in Example 2.3.4.

Example 2.3.4

```
> if (TRUE) { print('hi')}
[1] "hi"
```

In Example 2.3.5 and in the problems at the end of this chapter, you might be tempted to just look at the line of code and figure out what is wrong without looking at the error. That is almost always possible, and in fact easy, in isolated textbook examples. The point here is to give you practice reading and making sense of error messages so that when the context is much more complicated and you really are feeling stuck, writing your own code, or adapting someone else's, you can use the error message to help you get unstuck.

Example 2.3.5

```
> if {TRUE} print('hi')
Error: unexpected '{' in "if {"
```

The problem with Example 2.3.5 is, again, the braces around the expression after `if`. The fix is to use parentheses, as in Example 2.3.6.

Example 2.3.6

```
> if (TRUE) print('hi')
[1] "hi"
```

2.4 Indexing Errors

For this next example, 2.4.1, we have constructed

a vector of people's ages, with a name for each age.

Example 2.4.1

```
> myAges <- c(  19,    18,    21,    20)
> names(myAges) <- c('mary','sam',
                     'kim','bill')
> myAges
mary  sam  kim bill
  19   18   21   20
```

There are four things in the vector, `myAges`, so if we try to access the fifth, we get an error (Example 2.4.2).

Example 2.4.2

```
> myAges[[5]]
Error in myAges[[5]] : subscript out of
bounds
```

We also get the same kind of error if we use a name as an index, but misspell it, even if it is a very minor misspelling, like using a capital letter instead of lowercase one, as shown in Example 2.4.3.

Example 2.4.3

```
> myAges[['Sam']]
Error in myAges[["Sam"]] : subscript out
of bounds
```

The names in our vector, `myAges`, are all uncapitalized. When we capitalize `Sam`, we get the same result as if we had asked for any other unknown name. The error message `subscript out of bounds` is quite helpful. It tells you that there is a mismatch between what you are trying to retrieve, and what is actually there. Note here we are using the double brackets (`[[]]`), which retrieve a single element. We get a different behavior if we use the single brackets, which retrieve a range of values. When we try to extract the fifth value, shown in Example 2.4.4, using only single brackets, we get what may be unexpected behavior, but no error.

Example 2.4.4

```
> myAges[5]
 <NA>
  NA
```

```
> myAges['Sam']
 <NA>
   NA
```

In this case R is behaving as if there is, or could be, a fifth element to `myAges`, but it has no value yet. It is returning a value that is a one-element numeric vector, with the value being `NA` and the name of that position in the vector being `NA`, too. `NA` is R's way of indicating a missing value.

When there is an `NA` in a character vector, it often gets printed as `<NA>` to distinguish it from the possibility that you actually have a legitimate value spelled `NA`.

It is extremely easy to make a mistake of the sort in Example 2.4.2, 2.4.3, or 2.4.4, by typing `jim` when you meant `kim`, or `Mary` when you meant `mary`, or `MyAges` when you meant `myAges`. The errors can be difficult to spot if, instead of our tiny example with four names, you have twenty or a hundred or more, especially if you are using real data that someone else produced, and you are not familiar with the names. These also happen if you are mixing different naming styles, like `myAges` versus `my.ages` versus `MyAges`.

In the next section, I introduce two extremely helpful functions for finding such mistakes, once you have realized you probably have a name mismatch from a typo.

2.5 The Functions setdiff and agrep

For this section, and the accompanying exercises at the end of the chapter, we will use some built-in data sets: `USJudgeRatings` and `mtcars`.

`USJudgeRatings` has 43 rows, each for a different judge, and 12 columns, each for a different criterion. Example 2.5.1 shows the first 12 rows of the data set. The data include lawyers' ratings of certain state judges from a 1977 *New Haven Register* article using data provided by John Hartigan. Examples of the headings are `INTG` for the judges' integrity, `DILG` for diligence, and `DECI` for how prompt the judges' decisions were.

Example 2.5.1

```
> USJudgeRatings[1:12, 1:12]
                CONT INTG DMNR DILG CFMG DECI PREP FAMI ORAL WRIT PHYS RTEN
AARONSON,L.H.    5.7  7.9  7.7  7.3  7.1  7.4  7.1  7.1  7.1  7.0  8.3  7.8
ALEXANDER,J.M.   6.8  8.9  8.8  8.5  7.8  8.1  8.0  8.0  7.8  7.9  8.5  8.7
ARMENTANO,A.J.   7.2  8.1  7.8  7.8  7.5  7.6  7.5  7.5  7.3  7.4  7.9  7.8
BERDON,R.I.      6.8  8.8  8.5  8.8  8.3  8.5  8.7  8.7  8.4  8.5  8.8  8.7
BRACKEN,J.J.     7.3  6.4  4.3  6.5  6.0  6.2  5.7  5.7  5.1  5.3  5.5  4.8
BURNS,E.B.       6.2  8.8  8.7  8.5  7.9  8.0  8.1  8.0  8.0  8.0  8.6  8.6
CALLAHAN,R.J.   10.6  9.0  8.9  8.7  8.5  8.5  8.5  8.5  8.6  8.4  9.1  9.0
```

```
COHEN,S.S.       7.0 5.9 4.9 5.1 5.4 5.9 4.8 5.1 4.7 4.9 6.8 5.0
DALY,J.J.        7.3 8.9 8.9 8.7 8.6 8.5 8.4 8.4 8.4 8.5 8.8 8.8
DANNEHY,J.F.     8.2 7.9 6.7 8.1 7.9 8.0 7.9 8.1 7.7 7.8 8.5 7.9
DEAN,H.H.        7.0 8.0 7.6 7.4 7.3 7.5 7.1 7.2 7.1 7.2 8.4 7.7
DEVITA,H.J.      6.5 8.0 7.6 7.2 7.0 7.1 6.9 7.0 7.0 7.1 6.9 7.2
```

In Example 2.5.2, we attempt to extract some of the columns of the fifth row of `USJudgeRatings`, in a slightly different order, and something goes wrong.

Example 2.5.2

```
> USJudgeRatings[ 5, c('DECI',
'ORAL', 'PREP', 'WRIT', 'DILG',
'RTEN', 'DNMR', 'INTG', 'FAMI',
'CFMG', 'PHYS', 'CONT')]

Error in
`[.data.frame`(USJudgeRatings, 5,
c("DECI", "ORAL", "PREP", "WRIT", :
   undefined columns selected
```

Before we try to parse the error message, we need to understand this bit: `` `[.data.frame` ``. This odd-looking thing is the name of the function that is called when you want to retrieve some rows and columns from a data frame, which is a particular kind of data structure in R. (The back-ticks (`) at both ends tell us R is treating it as a symbol.) If we just wanted to retrieve the first three rows and columns of a data frame, we could do it with brackets ([]) or with `` `[.data.frame` ``, as shown in Example 2.5.3. In fact, either way, the odd-looking function `` `[.data.frame` `` ends up being called.

Example 2.5.3

```
> USJudgeRatings[1:3, 1:3]
                CONT INTG DMNR
AARONSON,L.H.    5.7  7.9  7.7
ALEXANDER,J.M.   6.8  8.9  8.8
ARMENTANO,A.J.   7.2  8.1  7.8

> `[.data.frame`(USJudgeRatings,1:3,1:3)
                CONT INTG DMNR
AARONSON,L.H.    5.7  7.9  7.7
ALEXANDER,J.M.   6.8  8.9  8.8
ARMENTANO,A.J.   7.2  8.1  7.8
```

Now we can parse the error message in Example 2.5.2. We have an error in our function call to retrieve some rows and columns from the data frame, `USJudgeRatings`, and we are told we have some "`undefined columns selected`." Based on the error, it is likely that one of the column names is misspelled. You might try to compare the names in your code with the actual names simply by printing them both out, and looking at them, as shown in Example 2.5.4.

Example 2.5.4

First we show the actual column names:

```
> colnames(USJudgeRatings)
 [1] "CONT" "INTG" "DMNR" "DILG"
 [5] "CFMG" "DECI" "PREP" "FAMI"
 [9] "ORAL" "WRIT" "PHYS" "RTEN"
```

Here is the list containing the mistake:

```
c( 'DECI', 'ORAL', 'PREP', 'WRIT',
'DILG', 'RTEN', 'DNMR', 'INTG',
'FAMI', 'CFMG', 'PHYS', 'CONT')
```

That might work, but it also might take a long time and give you a headache. There is a quicker, more systematic way. There are two steps. The first step is shown in Example 2.5.5, where we look for elements of the column names in our code, that are not in the set of actual column names, using the set difference function, `setdiff`. The first argument is the vector of column names in our code. The second is the actual column names. We want to know which of our names are not in the real set.

Example 2.5.5

```
> setdiff(c('DECI', 'ORAL', 'PREP', 'WRIT',
            'DILG', 'RTEN', 'DNMR', 'INTG',
            'FAMI', 'CFMG', 'PHYS', 'CONT'),
          colnames(USJudgeRatings))
[1] "DNMR"
```

Example 2.5.5 shows that `"DNMR"` is in our set but not the real set. The second step in this process is to find out what the right column name is. At this point, you might be tempted to just eyeball the real set and spot and fix the problem, but if you have fifty or a hundred column names or more, that is suboptimal. For such a case, we use the function `agrep`. It does fuzzy matching. We know that `"DNMR"` is not in the real set of headers, and we want to know what `"DNMR"` is a misspelling of. In the code in Example 2.5.6, the `agrep` function will try to match (loosely)

"DNMR" to every item in the real set. There is an adjustable threshold for how closely to match. If at first you don't succeed, you can loosen the threshold by increasing the `max.distance`. On our third try, we succeed in finding a match, and the match is `"DMNR"`. That is, the `M` and `N` were transposed.

Example 2.5.6

```
> agrep( 'DNMR', names(USJudgeRatings))
integer(0)
> agrep( 'DNMR', names(USJudgeRatings),
        max.distance = 1)
integer(0)
> agrep( 'DNMR', names(USJudgeRatings),
        max.distance = 2)
[1] 3
> names(USJudgeRatings)[[3]]
[1] "DMNR"
```

The use of the two functions, `setdiff` and `agrep`, allowed us to systematically find our spelling mistake, transposing `M` and `N`. For simple, small problems, being systematic like this can be overkill, but you now have the tools and the choice.

2.6 Exercises

In the lines of code below, you are asked to predict whether something will go wrong, and if so, roughly what that is. If you don't know, an easy way to find out is to try the code out. In the answers given in Section 2.7, there is sometimes additional explanatory detail. The lines of code start with R's prompt (>). The code we are asking about comes to the right of the prompt.

Exercise 2.1. The line below produces an error involving either the words "not found" or "unexpected." Which phrase is it, and why?

```
> .
```

Exercise 2.2. The line below also produces an error. This looks almost the same as the line in the preceding exercise. The error for this line involves either the phrase "not found" or the word "unexpected." Which is it?

```
> ,
```

Exercise 2.3. For Exercises 2.1 and 2.2, why do the period and the comma produce such different errors?

Exercise 2.4. Does the next line of code produce a warning, or an error? What is wrong? Does the output contain "not found" or "unexpected?"

```
> paste('myFirstBit',  `MySecondBit`)
```

Exercise 2.5. In this line of code, is there an error, a warning, or a value returned? If there is a value returned, what is it? If an error or warning, which of these two words/phrases, "not found" or "unexpected," is output?

```
> paste('myFirstBit', 'MySecondBit') ==
  "MyFirstBit MySecondBit"
```

Exercise 2.6. Does this line of code print something, or produce an error? If it works, what is the value, and if not, do the words "unexpected" or "not found" appear in the error?

```
> make_hpc_pbs_files <- function
    (arglist=list(c(.05,.1), c(.2,.2))
    print(arglist[[1]])
```

Exercise 2.7. This next line looks very similar to the line in the previous exercise, but is slightly different. Does this line of code print something, or produce an error? If it works, what is the value, and if not, do the words "unexpected" or "not found" appear in the error?

```
> make_hpc_pbs_files <- function
   (arglist= list(c(.05,.1),c(.2,.2))
   {print(arglist[[1]])}}
```

Exercise 2.8. Assume neither `a` nor `b` has a value. Predict and compare the errors in these two lines.

```
> a <- b
> a < - b
```

Exercise 2.9. This line of code produces an error:

```
> USJudgeRatings[ 3, c('DMNR', 'FAMI',
  'DECI', 'INTG', 'PHYS', 'PERP', 'CONT',
  'GFMC', 'ORAL', 'DILG', 'RTEN', 'WRIT')]
```

More than one of the indices are misspelled. Use the techniques from Section 2.5 involving `agrep` and `setdiff` to find the errors. Which terms were misspelled? What should they have been? How large did you need to make the parameter `max.distance`?

Exercise 2.10. There is a built-in data set called `mtcars`, with 32 rows and 11 columns. It's from a 1974 issue of *Motor Trend.* Here I'm showing just a few of the middle rows of the data set.

```
> mtcars[23:28,]
                  mpg cyl  disp  hp drat    wt  qsec vs am gear carb
AMC Javelin      15.2   8 304.0 150 3.15 3.435 17.30  0  0    3    2
Camaro Z28       13.3   8 350.0 245 3.73 3.840 15.41  0  0    3    4
Pontiac Firebird 19.2   8 400.0 175 3.08 3.845 17.05  0  0    3    2
Fiat X1-9        27.3   4  79.0  66 4.08 1.935 18.90  1  1    4    1
Porsche 914-2    26.0   4 120.3  91 4.43 2.140 16.70  0  1    5    2
Lotus Europa     30.4   4  95.1 113 3.77 1.513 16.90  1  1    5    2
```

The line below attempts to extract some information about the Porsche, Camaro, and Fiat, but there are errors in both the row and column indices.

```
> mtcars[c('Porsche 914-2','Fiat X1-9',
           'Camaro 2Z8'),
           c('mpg', 'hp ', 'drat')]
```

Find the misspelled items. You will need the functions `colnames`, `rownames`, and `setdiff`.

Exercise 2.11. Each of the names in this vector:

```
c('DONNEHY', 'GRILO', 'RUBINOV',
  'ARONSON', 'SANTANIELLO')
```

is a misspelling of a judge's name from the `USJudgeRatings` data frame. Use `agrep` to find the correct spellings of the names.

2.7 Answers to Exercises

2.1 The error message is [`Error:object '.' not found`]. The dot is parsed as a symbol, i.e., a name of a variable that has no value in this case.

2.2 This line has a comma. The line in Exercise 2.1 has a period. The difference is always important, and usually not obvious. The error message is [`Error: unexpected ',' in ","`]. The comma is a separator and cannot be a function or a variable. Since a comma separates two things, one of them needs to have occurred already.

2.3 A period (`.`) is just like any other alphabetic character to R, so it is treated like a symbol, i.e., a name for an object. But a comma (`,`) is a crucial part of R's syntax. It is a separator.

2.4 The backticks around `MySecondBit` cause it to be parsed as a symbol. That means it will be treated as a variable in this context, but it has no value. There is an error:

```
Error in paste("myFirstBit",
  MySecondBit) :
  object 'MySecondBit' not found
```

That means R is trying to find the value of `MySecondBit`, but cannot.

2.5 There is no error or warning. The value is `FALSE`. Note that the `m` in `myFirstBit` is not capitalized, and the `M` in `MySecondBit` is. When we read, we often do not notice whether letters are capitalized. These errors can be hard to spot. Chapter 3 talks about ways to avoid making mistakes like this.

2.6 The error message is:

```
Error: unexpected symbol in
"make_hpc_pbs_files <- function
   (arglist= list(c(.05,.1),
    c(.2,.2))  print"
```

The error indicates there is something wrong by the time we get to `print`. The last thing quoted in the error message is the symbol `print`, and it is unexpected. That means that probably, there is a missing comma, or there are mismatched parentheses or braces. In this case, there needs to be one more right parenthesis (close parenthesis) before `print`. In Chapter 3, I show how a good editor can help find and prevent such mistakes.

2.7 The error is:

```
Error: unexpected '{'  in
"make_hpc_pbs_files <-
function (arglist= list(c(.05,.1),
       c(.2,.2)) {"
```

The unexpected left brace before `print` in the origial line of code indicates a missing comma, or mismatched delimiters. There needs to be an additional right parenthesis (close parenthesis) before the brace, to close `arglist`.

2.8 In the first line, `a <- b`, the error is:

```
Error: object 'b' not found
```

That is because the operation is assignment, and there is no value for `b`. There doesn't need to be a value for `a`.

In the second line, `a < - b`, the error is:

```
Error: object 'a' not found
```

We have a *less than* comparison in the second line, so there needs to be a value for `a`.

2.9 The misspelled items are: `'PERP'` and `'GFMC'`. They should be `'PREP'` and `'CFMG'`, respectively. In both cases, I set the parameter `max.distance` for `agrep` to be 2. Anything bigger than `1` seems to do the trick in this case.

2.10 `'hp '` has a space inside the quotes. `'Camaro 2Z8'` has the `Z` and the `2` transposed. Such errors are typically very difficult to find just by looking, hence the tools.

2.11 Here is some code using `agrep` for finding the misspellings:

```
> for (misspelling in
       c('DONNEHY', 'GRILO', 'RUBINOV',
        'ARONSON', 'SANTANIELLO'))
  {print( rownames(USJudgeRatings)[
   agrep(misspelling,
         rownames(USJudgeRatings),
         max.distance=1)])}
[1] "DANNEHY,J.F."
[1] "GRILLO,A.E."
[1] "RUBINOW,J.E."
[1] "AARONSON,L.H."
[1] "SATANIELLO,A.G."
```

Note that we cannot actually know beforehand that the code just given will work perfectly. `agrep` might have needed to be given a more relaxed value for `max.distance`. We got lucky.

Chapter 3

Lighten Your Cognitive Load

3.1 Upper- and Lowercase Letters

In reading and writing normal text, A and a are two different looks for the same letter. In R, they are different characters. You can have a function or variable called `Abc` and a different one called `abc`. They are different. For instance, R comes with two different built-in variables: `letters`, and `LETTERS`. The first is bound to a vector of lowercase letters, from a to z. The second is a vector of the uppercase letters from A to Z. If you want to use the vector of uppercase letters, and try to get them using the variable name `Letters` (capital L, the rest lowercase), you get an error message. By now, you should be able to predict what it is. Can you? It is `Error: object 'Letters' not found`. We humans have developed habits over a lifetime of reading that tell us that a capital A is the same letter as a lowercase a and a capital L is the same as a lowercase l. That habit represents a difference between how we use capital letters and the way R uses capital letters. Unfortunately for us humans, changing a habit is very different from learning a new fact. Now that you have been told that R treats upper- and lowercase letters as different, you know it. But your cognitive habit of seeing them as the same is not so easily changed.

If you are going to be using R with any degree of regularity, you will benefit from cultivating habits that preempt these kinds of mistakes. In the next section, I present an extremely useful editing tool, name completion, which can help you avoid making mistakes involving confusion of upper- and lowercase letters.

3.2 Completion of Filenames

Programs are full of names. They have variable names, function names, argument names, and often they refer to filenames and folder/directory names. If the names are very short, like `tmp`, `a`, `b`, or `foo`, they are not very informative, and so it can be hard to remember what they stand for. That puts a load on memory—the human programmer's memory. If they are much longer and informative, like `my-proteomic-data-with-lines-3-5-removed.csv`, their contents can be very easily remembered, but the exact spelling of the name can be nearly impossible to remember and type correctly.

In this next example (3.2.1), we'll go over how to use filename completion to resolve and avoid problems involving misspelling of filenames. In the example, we try to read a file of data with a misspelled filename.

Example 3.2.1

```
> dir()
[1] "my-proteomic-data-with-lines-3-
5-removed.csv"
```

```
> read.csv("my-proteomic-date-with-
lines-3-5-removed.csv")
Error in file(file, "rt") : cannot
open the connection
In addition: Warning message:
In file(file, "rt") :
  cannot open file 'my-proteomic-
date-with-lines-3-5-removed.csv': No
such file or directory
```

The error mentions two words that have special meanings, *connection* and *open*. *Connections* comprise a layer of infrastructure that gets used when programs try to read or write files. For now, all you really need to know about them is that when R reads or writes a file, a connection is involved. Prior to actually reading or writing a file, a connection needs to be opened. This is done by some function within the definition of `read.csv`.

Now let's read the error and try to make sense of it. The actual error says, `Error in file(file, "rt"): cannot open the connection`. This may be a little surprising. It looks like R thinks we invoked a function named `file` that has two arguments. The first is *also* called `file`, and the second is called `rt`. This function was either called from `read.csv`, or from some function that is part of the definition of `read.csv`, or from some function more deeply embedded in definitions of definitions. The next part of the message, shown in Example 3.2.2, is a little more helpful.

Example 3.2.2

```
In addition: Warning message:
In file(file, "rt") :
  cannot open file 'my-proteomic-
date-with-lines-3-5-removed.csv': No
such file or directory
```

When a file cannot be opened, there are four common reasons. One is that the filename was misspelled. Another is that there is a mismatch between the folder the file is in and where R thinks to look. And a third is that the file doesn't exist. For instance, maybe you intended to download it or move it to the right place, but have not done so yet. The last is that there can be read/write access constraints on files, and someone might not have permission to read or write the file. Here, we limit ourselves to the problem of misspelling. The other three have to do with understanding your computer's file system, and are beyond what I can explain here.

There are two very useful bits of information in the warning message. One is the actual full name of the file that R tried and failed to open. The other is that there is no file or directory spelled exactly that way. (*Directory* is another name for *folder*. Unix/Linux systems tend to use the word *directory* and Windows and Apple tend to use *folder*.)

The warning message did not tell us what the problem is, exactly. Even if we suspect a misspelling, our visual perceptual system is likely to see what we expect, namely the correct name. Finding the typo, if indeed that is the problem, can sometimes be frustratingly difficult. And that is why people build *completion* into their computer systems. In the R console window, the tab key on the keyboard performs name completion. The main reason to get into the habit of using completion is not to save a few keystrokes of typing. It is to avoid making time-consuming, frustrating mistakes. Typos are easy to make and can be tricky to find. A better way to read the file in Example 3.2.1 is shown in Example 3.2.3.

Example 3.2.3

```
> getwd()
```

This tells you where R will look for and write files. Make a file with the name

```
my-proteomic-data-with-
lines-3-5-removed.csv
```

and put it in this directory. Then, type

```
> read.csv('my')
```

and then, with the cursor right after the `y` in `my`, hit the tab key on the keyboard to complete the filename. That automatically completes as much as possible, and in our case we see this:

```
> read.csv('my-proteomic-data-with-
lines-3-5-removed.csv')
```

For some readers it will have been obvious what was wrong, for others, maybe not. The reason the file could not be opened was that we misspelled its name. We made a common typo, typing `date` instead of `data` in the middle of the filename.

The exact behavior of the tab depends on the system. In some systems, if there is more than one possible completion, a menu of options is displayed, and they can be navigated with up and down arrows on the keyboard, and selected with another tap of the tab key, or with the enter/return key. This is how RStudio (Windows, Mac, and Linux), Emacs with ESS (Windows, Mac, Linux), and the built-in R console on Mac function. It is worth experimenting, and then cultivating the habit of using completion. The exercises at the end of this chapter are formulated to help you develop these habits.

3.3 Completion: Variables and Functions

Completion works for variable and function names too. If we have defined two very long variables, `myNewDataVector`, `myolddatavector`, and a function, `my.elaborate.processing.fn`, we can use tab completion on them. In Example 3.3.1, we define two variables and a function, so we can illustrate how completion works on them.

Example 3.3.1

```
myNewDataVector <- c( 2, 1, 5, 1, 3, 5)
myolddatavector <- c( 2, 1, 5, 1, 3, 4)
my.elaborate.processing.fn <- function
(a) print(a)
```

In the R console, at the prompt (>), if we type `my` and then hit the tab key on the keyboard, we see a menu of the possible completions based on what has been defined already. In our case, we see these possible completions:

```
my.elaborate.processing.fn
myAges
myNewDataVector
myolddatavector
```

Did you notice that `myAges` also showed up? It was still there from when I defined it earlier.

Completion is much more than a convenience for typing. It is a tremendously useful human memory aid and error prevention device. If you keep your variable and function names short, it is hard to remember what they are for. Completion lets you use longer, more informative names, to aid your memory. Without completion, you could still use long names, but it would be difficult to remember how each one was spelled, and difficult to type them correctly, without errors. Moreover, completion does not just work for names you create.

Completion works for the names of functions and variables that come with R. There are many, many names, and within R, naming styles are not consistent. Sometimes R uses a dot between parts of a function name, like `set.seed`, but sometimes it doesn't, as in the functions `setwd` and `setdiff`. At times R uses camel case, where the word parts are capitalized, as in `readLines`, and at other times it doesn't, as in `readline`. Without the built-in completion functionality, remembering all these idiosyncracies would be a huge drain. Getting into the habit of using completion can spare you many frustrating moments down the line.

3.4 Matching Quotes

The completion function aids human memory. Our next sections talk about aids for human visual perception. Most people are not so good at finding mismatched delimiters: parentheses, brackets, braces, and quotes. Once again, there are tools available to aid us in the programming process. Example 3.4.1 contains code for extracting some rows and columns from the `mtcars` data set (mentioned earlier in Exercise 2.10), but in the example, something went wrong.

Example 3.4.1

```
> mtcars[ c('Porsche 914-2', 'Fiat
X1-9, 'Camaro Z28'), c('mpg', 'hp ',
'drat')]
Error: unexpected symbol in
"mtcars[ c('Porsche 914-2', 'Fiat X1-9,
'Camaro"
```

The error says there is an `unexpected symbol`, but we have all the right number of commas, parentheses, and brackets. The real problem, this time, is a missing single quote. Contrast Example 3.4.1 with Examples 3.4.2, 3.4.3, and 3.4.4. These examples show how three different R code editors use color to help you spot the mistake.

Example 3.4.2 RStudio editor:

```
mtcars[c("Porsche  914-2",
  "Fiat X1-9, "Camaro 2Z8"),
   c("mpg", "hp ", "drat")]
```

Example 3.4.3

Emacs with ESS:

```
mtcars[c("Porsche  914-2",
  "Fiat X1-9, "Camaro 2Z8"),
   c("mpg", "hp ", "drat")]
```

Example 3.4.4

Editor that comes bundled with R for Mac:

```
mtcars[c("Porsche  914-2",
  "Fiat X1-9, "Camaro 2Z8"),
   c("mpg", "hp ", "drat")]
```

In Example 3.4.2, the text within matching quotes is green. The other text is black. In Examples 3.4.3 and 3.4.4, the text within matching quotes is red. The other text is blue.

The fact that, in all three examples, `Camaro` is not the same color as the other cars indicates that it is not between matching quotes. In fact, the quote in front of `Camaro` closes the quote for `Fiat X1-9`. The error is that there should be an additional quote after `Fiat X1-9` and before the comma.

Most code editors will let you pick colors that work best for you, and there are many more code editors than the three listed in Examples 3.4.2, 3.4.3, and 3.4.4. In addition to helping with mismatched quotes, code editors can also help you avoid errors using two similar and extremely useful functionalities. When the cursor is on a parenthesis (or brace or bracket), they highlight the matching one. They also provide a way, with a keyboard command, to move the cursor forward or backward to the matching parenthesis (or brace or bracket). In RStudio, the command is control-p. In Emacs with ESS, you use control-alt-f (for forward) and control-alt-b (for backward) to move the cursor to the matching one. In the R console on my Mac, using the function key and arrow keys, the keyboard commands are function-$\leftarrow$ and function-$\rightarrow$.

3.5 Editing in the Console

The process of troubleshooting often involves executing some code, looking at the result, and then making some small change, and trying again. In RStudio and the basic R console, there are some very handy editing capabilities built in.

In the console, let's say you just evaluated some R code, and now you want to redo it, but with a small change. With the cursor at the very bottom of the console window, you can use the up and down arrows on the keyboard to navigate through the previous bits of code you have evaluated.

Suppose you have recently executed the bits of R code in Example 3.5.1.

Example 3.5.1

```
> rnorm(n=8,mean=500,sd=10)
[1] 511 515 500 505 510 504 496 498

> mtcars[1,1:4 ]
          mpg cyl disp  hp
Mazda RX4  21   6  160 110
```

```
> myAges
mary  sam  kim bill
  19   18   21   20
```

And then you realize you want to redo the generation of normal random numbers, because you want the mean to be 50, not 500. With the cursor at the bottom of the console, hitting the up arrow once produces the line

```
> myAges
```

Hitting the up arrow again produces the line

```
> mtcars[1,1:4 ]
```

And hitting it one more time produces the line

```
> rnorm(n=8,mean=500,sd=10)
```

At this point, you can edit the line, changing the 500 to 50. The built-in editing commands listed next may come in handy. In them, control is abbreviated as C-, so, for instance, C-a means hold down the control key and type a.

Here are some useful built-in commands for editing in the console:

- C-a moves the cursor to the beginning of the line (mnemonic: ***a*** is at the beginning of the alphabet)
- C-e moves the cursor to the ***e***nd of the line
- Use C-k to cut and save up to the end of a line (mnemonic: ***k***ill to the end of the line)
- C-y ***y***anks back (i.e., pastes) the "killed" piece (from C-k)

3.6 Exercises

Exercise 3.1. R has a function called `readline` (singular, lowercase), and another one (plural, camel case) called `readLines`. Find out whether there is a `readLine` function (camel case, singular). Use completion.

Exercise 3.2. How many functions start with the string `read.f`? Use completion to find out.

Exercise 3.3. There is a function that is useful for debugging. It is called either `browse` or `browser`. Use completion to find out which it is.

Exercise 3.4. For two vectors, `A` and `B`, suppose you need to know whether they contain the same numbers, just in different orders, or whether they contain different numbers.

```
> A <- c(4,  6,  8, 11,  3,  9, 10,
14,  5,  1,  2, 13, 12, 15,  7)

> B <- c(8, 11, 13,  5,  9, 10,  2,
6,  1, 14, 15,  7, 12,  3,  4)
```

Use completion to look for a function that can tell you whether two *sets* are *equal*. Use it to compare `A` and `B`.

Exercise 3.5. There is a useful data set built into R called `iris`. Use completion to find out if there are any other data sets whose names start with `iris`.

3.7 Answers to Exercises

3.1 No.

3.2 There are three: `read.fortran`, `read.ftable`, and `read.fwf`.

3.3 `browser`

3.4 The function is named `setequal`.

```
> setequal(A,B)
[1] TRUE
```

3.5 Yes, there is also a data frame called `iris3`.

Chapter 4

Brackets All the Way Down

4.1 Principles for Indexing

In R, a fundamentally important notion is that of subsequence. R is built around this notion, and once you understand it, you will have way fewer problems. A very useful, but also misleading and confusing fact about the way R does things, is that a subsequence that starts and ends with the ith element is the same as the ith element. This is a little like saying that the vector containing the number 3 is the same as the number 3. We'll explore this in Example 4.1.1.

Example 4.1.1

```
> 4[1][1][1][1] == 4
[1] TRUE
> 5[[1]][[1]][[1]]
[1] 5

> identical(5[1], 5)
[1] TRUE
> identical(5[[1]], 5)
[1] TRUE
```

Example 4.1.1 shows that a number like 4 or 5 is treated exactly like a vector consisting of one number. So the subsequence consisting of the first element is that number. Also, using double brackets to extract a single element still just gives back the original number. Lists are sometimes treated the same way, but not exactly, as shown in Example 4.1.2.

Example 4.1.2

```
> list(3) == 3
[1] TRUE
```

```
> identical(list(3), 3)
[1] FALSE
```

This way of treating numbers as vectors can be a little confusing, but it also means that you can often get away with being a little bit sloppy in how you do indexing. See Examples 4.1.3 and 4.1.4.

Example 4.1.3

```
> myAges <- c(19, 18, 21, 20)
> names(myAges) <- c('mary', 'sam',
                     'kim', 'bill')
> myAges
mary  sam  kim bill
  19   18   21   20
```

The way R does indexing means that `myAges[3]` is the same as `myAges[[3]]`, and both are the same as `myAges[['kim']]`.

Example 4.1.4

```
> myAges[[3]] == myAges[3]
 kim
TRUE
```

```
> myAges[3] == myAges['kim']
 kim
TRUE
> myAges[3] == myAges[['kim']]
 kim
TRUE
```

The way numbers are treated as vectors may be unexpected, and can lead to confusion or errors until you understand what is happening behind the scenes. Another example of something hidden that can lead to errors in indexing is described in the next section.

4.2 Operator Precedence

Here is one kind of indexing error that can be hard to spot. Say you want a loop to start at a=1, and go to b+1.

```
> a <- 1
> b <- 3
```

You might want a loop like this:

```
> for (i in a:(b+1)) {do_something()}
```

Note that in this formulation, the loop index `i` will take on the values you want. Here's how you can check:

```
> a:(b+1)
```

```
[1] 1 2 3 4
```

That might be what you want, but as you are deep in thought about the other complexities of the program, you might omit a pair of parentheses and write this:

```
> for (i in a:b+1) {do_something()}
```

Later, when you test it, you'll notice the loop isn't starting where you told it to, namely `a=1`. You'll look at the code you wrote and not see anything wrong. It sure looks to you like `i` should take on the values `1,2,3,4`. If it occurs to you to question what looks obviously right, you can try this:

```
> a:b+1
```

```
[1] 2 3 4
```

So if you think to try that test, you will instantly see, at least, where the problem is. What goes on behind the scenes is this. It turns out that R needs to make a decision about how tightly operators bind to their arguments. Most of us learn a little about this when we struggle with algebra for the first time. There are conventions about these things. For instance, $2 + 3 \times 4$ is taken by convention to mean $2 + (3 \times 4)$, even though we are all tempted to go in order from left to right and add the 2 to the 3 first. We are told that multiplication binds more tightly, or comes first.

It turns out that in R, there is a similar issue for the colon (`:`) and the plus sign (`+`), and the colon takes precedence. Hence we get that `a:b+1` is `2,3,4`, and not `1,2,3,4`. That is, `a:b` is `1,2,3`. Adding `1` to a vector is the same as adding `1` to each element of the vector, and that gives `2,3,4`. If you have written a program with this mistake in it, you might just look at your output and instantly realize what happened.

On the other hand, it might be that no matter how much you look, you continually see the expression `a:b+1`, and go through a simple mental check, each time coming up with the same incorrect calculation, because we are terrible at seeing something different from what we both want and expect. In that case, you may need to start a more thorough course of debugging, which is coming up next.

Chapter 5

Troubleshooting Basics

5.1 Beginning Troubleshooting

Troubleshooting is like any activity involving skill. It is possible to develop and refine specific sub-skills. An analogy is a visit to the doctor. Before prescribing a treatment, the doctor sets about diagnosing what might be wrong. This involves making guesses about where the problem might be, and then poking you there, and seeing if it hurts. What you, as a patient, don't see is what the doctor is thinking about. She has a great deal of information in mind about how bodies work. She knows about the circulatory system, and the lymphatic system, and the digestive system, and so on, and while she's poking and prodding you she's thinking about which of the systems might have a problem. She is trying to narrow down where the problem might be. Through years of training, she has refined her diagnostic skills. In medicine, diagnosis is taken as something worth becoming skilled at. In contrast, in science and statistics, computing skills seem to be regarded as something that anybody should be able to pick up on their own. In a regression class, you might be taught various diagnostic techniques for investigating whether a particular model is the right one, but you are unlikely to be taught how to diagnose your programming problems. In fact, there are useful techniques and strategies that you might not arrive at on your own, and the goal of this section is to teach them to you.

When you troubleshoot an R program, you need to know about R's parts and systems in the same way as a doctor needs to know about a human body. R has packages and variables and functions and environments and so on, and it helps to know about them. Then there are the individual programs. If something went wrong in your particular program, you want to find out where. You initially will be tempted to jump straight to trying to guess what went wrong. That is usually a slower, more frustrating approach than finding out first where the problem is, and then figuring out what it is.

The first strategy I'll describe as divide and conquer. It is a kind of binary search:

1. Divide the code into two parts.

2. Figure out somehow in which of the two parts the problem occurred.

3. Repeat the process on the part that contains the problem.

4. Eventually find exactly where the problem is.

5.2 Troubleshooting a Simple Example

Let's start with a very short simple example of some code that doesn't work. The goal, once we notice it doesn't work, is to find where the problem is, then what it is, then how to fix it. There is a built-in variable, `letters`, that is a vector of the lowercase letters of the English alphabet. Let's imagine we want to get a subvector of the first few letters, and we are going to use them somehow later. We might have a simple program like this:

```
> x1 <- 1
> x2 <- 4
> letters(x1:x2)
Error: could not find function "letters"
```

We know there is a problem. We divide the code into two parts, ànd endeavor to find out whether the error is in the first part or the second part. Even before we do that, we should read and try to understand as much of the error message as we can. It's trying to be helpful. It says, `could not find function "letters"`. There are three crucial bits of information in this message. The first is that something couldn't be found. The second is that the thing that couldn't be found is a function. The third bit of information is that the function that couldn't be found is called `letters`. All this information could lead us straight to the answer, but for illustrative purposes, let's imagine we don't yet know what and where the problem is. The error message would probably lead us to suspect that the problem is in the third line. Based on that assumption, let's divide our program into two parts, where the first part is the first two lines, and the second part is the line with `letters`. Notice that so far, we suspect, but don't actually know, that the problem lies in the second part. We should check and make sure there is no problem in the first part, especially since it is easy in this case. We check `x1`.

```
> x1
[1] 1
```

The value of `x1` is `1`, just as we want. Similarly, we check `x2`.

```
> x2
[1] 4
```

The value of `x2` is what it should be. Now we are pretty sure the problem lies in the second part of our program, the line `letters(x1:x2)`. Once again, we divide our code into two parts. This time, let's choose `letters` as the first part, and `(x1:x2)` as the second part. Let's see whether R can find `letters`.

```
> letters
 [1] "a" "b" "c" "d" "e" "f" "g" "h" "i"
[10] "j" "k" "l" "m" "n" "o" "p" "q" "r"
[19] "s" "t" "u" "v" "w" "x" "y" "z"
```

Sure enough, R can find `letters`. That means the problem is in the second part, `(x1:x2)`. If we want to divide `(x1:x2)` into two parts, this could be a bit tricky. One thing we can do is try simplifying it to this: `letters(1:4)`, or even to this: `letters(1)`. Here are the responses:

```
> letters(1:4)
Error: could not find function "letters"
> letters(1)
Error: could not find function "letters"
```

The only way I can think of to simplify this even further is to remove everything from the parentheses.

```
> letters()
Error: could not find function "letters"
```

At this point, we have established there is no problem with `letters`, so there must be a problem with the parentheses. By now either it occurs to you that you should be using square brackets instead of parentheses, or you turn to one of the introductory online R textbooks, and read about vectors and subvectors. Once you think of using brackets, you check this:

```
> letters[1:4]
[1] "a" "b" "c" "d"
```

And when that works, you check this:

```
>  letters[x1:x2]
[1] "a" "b" "c" "d"
```

In the foregoing example, even though it was incredibly simple, we were able to successfully use the strategy of dividing the code into two parts, and checking which of them contained the error. We did that several times recursively, and did it even after we had narrowed the problem down to a single short line. Finally, we were down to `letters()`, where we knew there was no problem in the first part, so there had to be a problem with what was left, the parentheses. The binary search technique is simple and powerful but not obvious.

One clue that could have led us to the answer more quickly was that `letters` was being treated by R as a function. We might have found the problem more quickly if the error message had said, "Something isn't right. (1) It's possible that *letters* is a misspelling of something. (2) It's possible that you are using parentheses when you should be using brackets. (3) It's possible that you meant to define a function spelled this way: `letters`, but either haven't written it yet, or haven't loaded it yet. (4) It's possible you intended to load some package that contains the function `letters`, but haven't yet." It is good that the error messages are short, but there is a downside to brevity. Here are some things that are always worth checking, even if you have been using R for some time:

- Check the spelling, including capital letters and periods.

- Check the delimiters: parentheses, braces, brackets, colons, commas, single and double quotes, etc.

- Check the other nonalphabetic characters: minus signs, slashes, asterisks, etc.

- Check whether you saved the file of definitions before you loaded it.

5.3 Summary

We used the strategy of dividing the code into two parts, and systematically checking each part to see whether the error was in it. The example we used here was meant to be simple. In the next chapter, we work through a more complicated example, using a built-in function made for debugging.

Chapter 6

Advanced Debugging

6.1 Introduction

So far, in this book, I have aimed to demystify error messages, and explain how and why to use completion for hard-to-remember and easy-to-misspell names of things: functions, files, variables, and so on. I have also explained how R treats a number the same as being a one-element vector. And, I gave a simple example of the divide-and-conquer strategy for troubleshooting.

In this chapter, we'll work through a more complicated debugging example, and I'll illustrate how to find the error using one of R's built-in debugging functions, `browser`.

6.2 When Nothing Is Obvious

Sometimes when an error is encountered, you have no error message, just a function that produced a result that you think (or know) isn't right. In such a case, troubleshooting is often like a treasure hunt. You don't know exactly where to look and, usually, you don't even know exactly what you're looking for. The next example is meant to be such a case.

6.3 Some Functions to Debug

We start with some functions that are just complicated enough that it is not obvious what is going wrong, but are still relatively short and simple. The functions we will be debugging are shown in Example 6.3.1. They are explained in Section 6.4.

Example 6.3.1

```
myPi <- function (n) {
    # Compute each term up to nth,
```

```
    # and add it to a cumulative sum.
    result <- 0
    for (k in 0:n) {
        result <- result + myPiFormula(k)
    }
    4 * result}

myPiFormula <- function (k) {
    # Compute the kth term.
    top <- (-1^k)
    bottom <- (2 * k  + 1)
    term <- top / bottom
#    browser()
}
```

6.4 What the Functions (Should) Do

The functions in Example 6.3.1 add the terms in a mathematical sum formula. The result gets closer and closer to the number π, as you add more and more terms. Here's the formula:

$$\frac{\pi}{4} = 1 - \frac{1}{3} + \frac{1}{5} - \frac{1}{7} + \frac{1}{9} - \cdots = \sum_{k=0}^{\infty} \frac{(-1)^k}{2k+1}.$$

I apologize to the reader for using a math formula that may not be familiar. I needed something that was a little bit complicated in order to illustrate the debugging. The math formula was the best thing I could come up with.

Our functions compute the sum for the first $n+1$ terms of the formula, from $k=0$ to $k=n$. As we add more and more terms, the sum should get closer to the value of π: 3.14159... There is at least one thing wrong in these functions, possibly more than one thing. We'll go over how to investigate whether the function seems to be giving the right answer, and if not, how to investigate further.

6.5 Start by Trying It Out

The first step is easy. Load the functions, and call the top-level one with a few different inputs, as shown in Example 6.5.1.

Example 6.5.1

```
> myPi(10)
[1] -8.723498
```

```
> myPi(50)
[1] -11.7907
> myPi(500)
[1] -16.36023
```

Okay, so we tried out the function, and it doesn't seem to be putting out numbers close to 3.14. Something is probably wrong. It might be tempting to jump to conclusions, but this section is about being *systematic* in looking for the problem.

6.6 What Is the Function Actually Doing?

It's common at this point to stare at the function definition and try to figure out what is going wrong. In our systematic approach, however, we start by looking at what is going on in the function. There is a built-in function for this purpose, `browser`. We add a call to the function `browser` in the definition of `myPiFormula`, at the end, and reload the definition. In Example 6.3.1, the call to `browser` is commented out with the hashtag. We remove the hashtag and reload the definition.

We call the function again to show how to use the function `browser` (Example 6.6.1).

Example 6.6.1

```
> myPi(10)
Called from: myPiFormula(k)
Browse[1]>
```

The function `myPi` executes the various commands in its definition until it comes to `browser`. At that point, the execution stops and waits for input from you. The first bit of input we will give it is to type "help" to get it to tell us what kinds of things we can do (Example 6.6.2).

Example 6.6.2

```
> myPi(10)
Called from: myPiFormula(k)
Browse[1]> help
n          next
s          step into
f          finish
c or cont  continue
Q          quit
where      show stack
help       show help
```

```
<expr>     evaluate expression
Browse[1]>
```

At this point, I would evaluate the function's variables `k, top, bottom,` and `term`, just to get an idea what's going on. See Example 6.6.3.

Example 6.6.3

```
> myPi(10)
Called from: myPiFormula(k)
Browse[1]> c(k, top, bottom, term)
[1]  0 -1  1 -1
```

Let's say those numbers don't make it obvious what's going on. If we type `f` for "finish," the function resumes executing normally until it gets to the call to `browser` again. Let's do that a few more times, and see what happens (Example 6.6.4).

Example 6.6.4

```
> myPi(10)
Called from: myPiFormula(k)
Browse[1]> c(k, top, bottom, term)
[1]  0 -1  1 -1
Browse[1]> f
```

```
Called from: myPiFormula(k)
Browse[1]> c(k, top, bottom, term)
[1]  1.0000 -1.0000
[3]  3.0000 -0.3333
Browse[1]> f
Called from: myPiFormula(k)
Browse[1]> c(k, top, bottom, term)
[1]  2.0 -1.0  5.0 -0.2
Browse[1]> f
Called from: myPiFormula(k)
Browse[1]> c(k, top, bottom, term)
[1]  3.0000 -1.0000
[3]  7.0000 -0.1429
Browse[1]> f
Called from: myPiFormula(k)
Browse[1]> c(k, top, bottom, term)
[1]  4.0000 -1.0000
[3]  9.0000 -0.1111
Browse[1]> f
Called from: myPiFormula(k)
Browse[1]> c(k, top, bottom, term)
[1]  5.00000 -1.00000
[3] 11.00000 -0.09091
```

First of all, yes, visually parsing that output can

be a little tedious. Sometimes debugging is like that. Secondly, we still don't know what we're looking for; we'll just keep and eye out for anything that jumps out, maybe a pattern, or an anomaly.

The pattern I'm noticing for all these terms is that they are negative, but they are supposed to add up to π. If they keep on being negative, they can't add up to π. So that seems wrong. Yay! We may be onto something.

At this point, I go back and look at the (easy part) of the formula:

$$\frac{\pi}{4} = 1 - \frac{1}{3} + \frac{1}{5} - \frac{1}{7} + \frac{1}{9} - \cdots$$

Half of the terms in the formula are positive, but in the output we looked at, all of the terms are negative. In the output, all of the numerators, `top`, are -1, and the denominators, `bottom`, are just the (positive) odd numbers, $1, 3, 5, 7, 9, 11$. It's looking like there's something wrong with how we compute `top`. So, in the next section, let's look at the definition of `myPiFormula` where `top` is defined.

6.7 Checking a Suspicious Bit of Code

Here's the line: `top <- (-1^k)`. We can try out just this line, with different values for `k`. We don't need to set the value for `top`. We can just evaluate `(-1^k)` with different values for `k` (Example 6.7.1).

Example 6.7.1

```
> (-1^1); (-1^2); (-1^3); (-1^4); (-1^5)
[1] -1
[1] -1
[1] -1
[1] -1
[1] -1
```

It looks like the parentheses are not where they need to be. We retry with the parentheses tightly around -1 (Example 6.7.2).

Example 6.7.2

```
> (-1)^1; (-1)^2; (-1)^3; (-1)^4; (-1)^5
[1] -1
[1] 1
```

```
[1] -1
[1] 1
[1] -1
```

That seems to be the problem, so we edit the function `miPiFormula`, and try again (Example 6.7.3).

Example 6.7.3

```
myPiFormula <- function (k) {
    # Compute the kth term.
    top <- (-1)^k
    bottom <- (2 * k  + 1)
    term <- top / bottom
#     browser()
}
```

Note that we edit the function `myPiFormula`, but then we call the top-level function, `myPi`, as shown in Example 6.7.4.

Example 6.7.4

```
> myPi(10)
[1] 3.232316
> myPi(50)
[1] 3.161199
```

```
> myPi(500)
[1] 3.143589
```

So we seem to have found and fixed the problem. Yay!

In debugging, figuring out *where* things are going wrong is usually the hard part. In this chapter, we've gone over how to use one of R's built-in functions that is made for debugging: `browser`. There is a more brute-force way to go, which is to put `print` statements in the function, wherever you think it might be helpful.

Sometimes it is possible to systematically divide the program in half, and check which part the error is in, and then repeat on that half. Other times, as in the current example, we don't know what we are looking for, so we start looking for a pattern or anomaly that might tell us where to look further. The function `browser` can be very helpful in that endeavor.

Chapter 7

Seeing the Invisible

7.1 The Read–Eval–Print Loop

We interact with R through a read–eval–print loop (REPL). We type or paste some text into the R console. R *reads* the text, *evaluates* it, and *prints* something about the result (usually).

It is worth it to understand a little about how the REPL works. In particular, when it prints something, is it the value returned by something that was just evaluated, or something else? If it was something else, why did it do that? And what was the actual result? There are a few different scenarios to understand.

Sometimes R evaluates the input and prints the result, as in Example 7.1.1.

Example 7.1.1

```
> 2+3
[1] 5

> cos(60 * pi/180)
[1] 0.5
```

Even here, though, R didn't *just* print the result. It also printed, before the result, `[1]`. That really isn't terribly helpful when the output is just a number. Example 7.1.2 shows how the REPL's addition to the value can be helpful.

Example 7.1.2

```
> letters
 [1] "a" "b" "c" "d" "e"
 [6] "f" "g" "h" "i" "j"
[11] "k" "l" "m" "n" "o"
[16] "p" "q" "r" "s" "t"
[21] "u" "v" "w" "x" "y"
[26] "z"
```

In Example 7.1.2, the value returned is a character vector with 26 lowercase letters. Each line of the REPL output begins with an index showing where in the vector this bit of output comes from. For instance, "k" is the 11th element of the vector, and "u" is the 21st.

Sometimes the REPL prints these useful indices when the value returned is a vector. But sometimes it doesn't. Example 7.1.3 shows how the printing of the value returned by an assignment function gets suppressed, unless the assignment is enclosed in parentheses.

Example 7.1.3

```
> a <- c(3,4,5)
>
> (a <- c(3,4,5))
[1] 3 4 5
> b <- (a <- c(3,4,5) + 5)
>
> b
[1]  8  9 10
>
```

Example 7.1.3 shows two things. One is the suppression of the printing of the value. The other is that even though assignment expressions don't usually have their value printed by the REPL, they still do return a value. The last bit of Example 7.1.3 shows `b` getting a value from the expression that assigns a value to `a`.

7.2 The Function invisible

There are other functions for which the REPL does not print out the value returned. This is accomplished by using the function `invisible`, as shown in Example 7.2.1.

Example 7.2.1

```
> invisible(3)
>
> invisible(3) + 4
[1] 7
```

7.3 Regression and the Function str

The functions for doing regression and analysis of variance print out lots of information, but they use `invisible` to suppress their actual returned value. If you want to get access to the actual data structure, you can, and you can use the function `str` to parse it; it'll help you extract exactly what you need (Example 7.3.1).

Example 7.3.1

```
> mydf
  x     y
1 1  9.37
2 2 20.18
3 3 29.16
> (myresult <- lm(y~x,mydf))

Call:
lm(formula = y ~ x, data = mydf)

Coefficients:
(Intercept)
     -0.217
          x
      9.895
```

As shown in Example 7.3.2, the entire result from the regression in Example 7.3.1 can be seen with the function `str`. There is no need to look at it in detail. The main points here are that some functions produce lots of potentially useful output, but don't put it all out there on the console, and that the function `str` can help you understand it if you ever need to.

Example 7.3.2

```
> str(myresult)
List of 12
 $ coefficients : Named num [1:2] -0.217 9.895
  ..- attr(*, "names")= chr [1:2] "(Intercept)" "x"
 $ residuals    : Named num [1:3] -0.305 0.61 -0.305
  ..- attr(*, "names")= chr [1:3] "1" "2" "3"
 $ effects      : Named num [1:3] -33.903 -13.994 -0.747
  ..- attr(*, "names")= chr [1:3] "(Intercept)" "x" ""
 $ rank         : int 2
 $ fitted.values: Named num [1:3] 9.68 19.57 29.47
  ..- attr(*, "names")= chr [1:3] "1" "2" "3"
 $ assign       : int [1:2] 0 1
 $ qr           :List of 5
  ..$ qr   : num [1:3, 1:2] -1.732 0.577 0.577 -3.464 -1.414 ...
  .. ..- attr(*, "dimnames")=List of 2
  .. .. ..$ : chr [1:3] "1" "2" "3"
  .. .. ..$ : chr [1:2] "(Intercept)" "x"
  .. ..- attr(*, "assign")= int [1:2] 0 1
  ..$ qraux: num [1:2] 1.58 1.26
  ..$ pivot: int [1:2] 1 2
  ..$ tol  : num 1e-07
  ..$ rank : int 2
  ..- attr(*, "class")= chr "qr"
 $ df.residual  : int 1
 $ xlevels      : Named list()
 $ call         : language lm(formula = y ~ x, data = mydf)
 $ terms        :Classes 'terms', 'formula'  language y ~ x
  .. ..- attr(*, "variables")= language list(y, x)
  .. ..- attr(*, "factors")= int [1:2, 1] 0 1
  .. .. ..- attr(*, "dimnames")=List of 2
  .. .. .. ..$ : chr [1:2] "y" "x"
  .. .. .. ..$ : chr "x"
  .. ..- attr(*, "term.labels")= chr "x"
  .. ..- attr(*, "order")= int 1
  .. ..- attr(*, "intercept")= int 1
  .. ..- attr(*, "response")= int 1
  .. ..- attr(*, ".Environment")=<environment: R_GlobalEnv>
  .. ..- attr(*, "predvars")= language list(y, x)
  .. ..- attr(*, "dataClasses")= Named chr [1:2] "numeric" "numeric"
  .. .. ..- attr(*, "names")= chr [1:2] "y" "x"
 $ model        :'data.frame':       3 obs. of  2 variables:
  ..$ y: num [1:3] 9.37 20.18 29.16
```

```
  ..$ x: int [1:3] 1 2 3
  ..- attr(*, "terms")=Classes 'terms', 'formula'  language y ~ x
  .. .. ..- attr(*, "variables")= language list(y, x)
  .. .. ..- attr(*, "factors")= int [1:2, 1] 0 1
  .. .. .. ..- attr(*, "dimnames")=List of 2
  .. .. .. .. ..$ : chr [1:2] "y" "x"
  .. .. .. .. ..$ : chr "x"
  .. .. ..- attr(*, "term.labels")= chr "x"
  .. .. ..- attr(*, "order")= int 1
  .. .. ..- attr(*, "intercept")= int 1
  .. .. ..- attr(*, "response")= int 1
  .. .. ..- attr(*, ".Environment")=<environment: R_GlobalEnv>
  .. .. ..- attr(*, "predvars")= language list(y, x)
  .. .. ..- attr(*, "dataClasses")= Named chr [1:2] "numeric" "numeric"
  .. .. .. ..- attr(*, "names")= chr [1:2] "y" "x"
 - attr(*, "class")= chr "lm"
```

If we ever want to, we can extract useful bits from the regression result, now that `str` has shown us what's there. For instance, if we want the coefficients, we would get them, as shown in Example 7.3.3.

Example 7.3.3

```
> myresult[["coefficients"]]
(Intercept)            x
     -0.217        9.895
> myresult$coefficients
(Intercept)            x
     -0.217        9.895
> myresult$coef
(Intercept)            x
     -0.217        9.895
```

```
> options(digits=8)
> myresult$coef
(Intercept)           x
-0.21697156  9.89541260
```

Example 7.3.3 shows a few different ways to extract the coefficients. The last bit of the example shows how to get more (or less) precision, if you want it, with the function `options(width=n)`.

7.4 The Function dput

There is one more useful function for when there's a discrepancy between what the R console shows you, and what it does. When `str` is not enough, sometimes the function `dput` can help.

Sometimes R does things that just look wrong. In Example 7.4.1, it looks like R correctly adds 1 to a million (10^6), but not to a trillion (10^{12}). What's up with that?

Example 7.4.1

```
> 1e6 + 1
[1] 1000001
> 1e12+1
[1] 1e+12
```

When you look deeper, with the function **dput** in Example 7.4.2, it turns out R did the right calculation, but made an assumption about how to print the result. The function **dput** prints out a value in such a way that R can read it back in correctly. But the function can also be helpful for understanding when things don't look right.

Example 7.4.2

```
> dput(1e12 +1)
1000000000001
```

Chapter 8

Conclusion

So far, we have covered lots of basic stuff for finding and fixing errors, and for avoiding them in the first place. We covered error messages, and how to let them help you. We covered ways of doing completion of names. I pointed out the way R treats a number as a vector, and treats an element of a vector as a subsequence.

In addition, we covered two different strategies for finding an error: divide-and-conquer, recursively eliminating parts of the code as possibly containing the error, and using `browser` to see what the code is doing, and looking for a pattern or anomaly.

Finally, we covered the read–eval–print loop, and the functions `invisible`, `str`, and `dput`, for when there is a mismatch between what R prints to the console, and what it has done behind the scenes.

The point here is that I have provided a good start for how to debug R code, but there is still more to know, especially about data structures. There are many excellent books on more advanced aspects of R, but those aspects are beyond the scope of this little book.

www.ingramcontent.com/pod-product-compliance
Lightning Source LLC
Chambersburg PA
CBHW050513210326
41521CB00011B/2440

* 9 7 9 8 9 9 4 4 5 4 6 0 2 *